This journal belongs to

Katie McMichael

ISBN 978-1-64352-762-8

Published by Barbour Publishing, Inc., 1810 Barbour Drive, Uhrichsville, Ohio 44683, www.barbourbooks.com

Our mission is to inspire the world with the life-changing message of the Bible.

 Member of the
Evangelical Christian
Publishers Association

Printed in China.

Donna K. Maltese

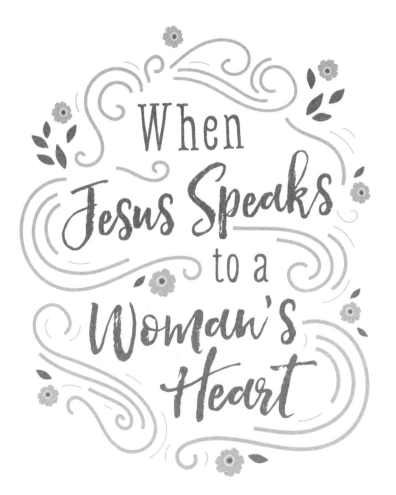

When Jesus Speaks to a Woman's Heart

Devotional Journal

BARBOUR
PUBLISHING

Introduction

There is no doubt that in today's society, women "belonging to the Way" (Acts 9:2 AMP) can use all the support they can get to keep themselves whole, healthy, and holy on the narrow but joy-filled road. Hence, the book you now hold in your hands—*When Jesus Speaks to a Woman's Heart*—was written with you in mind.

The readings that follow will quench your spiritual thirst, uplift your sometimes bruised and battered heart, and give you more power and strength as you continue on your divine journey. Covering matters such as finances, worries, woes, dreams, priorities, and love, you will find encouragement, direction, and inspiration. Each devotion acts as a reminder that a woman is first and foremost on Jesus' mind and that there is no broken heart He cannot heal, no strength He cannot imbue, and no miracle He cannot perform.

Permit these pages to draw you closer to Jesus, and explore

- His presence in your life.
- His passion to save you.
- His plea for you to love and accept yourself as you are today.
- His purpose to empower you.
- His plan to help you become who you were meant to be.

"The LORD bless you, and keep you [protect you, sustain you, and guard you]; the LORD make His face shine upon you [with favor], and be gracious to you [surrounding you with lovingkindness]; the LORD lift up His countenance (face) upon you [with divine approval], and give you peace [a tranquil heart and life]."
NUMBERS 6:24–26 AMP

Just Outside Your Door

I am standing just outside your door, only a breath, a prayer, a sigh away. Are your ears open to the sound of My knock? Will you open the door of your heart, mind, and soul to the light of My presence?

Allow the noises and the distractions, within and without, to fade away. Come to Me for the peace that this world cannot give. Then you will hear My tap, tap, tapping. Then you will relax and listen to what I have to say. As you heed My voice, barriers between you and Me dissolve. The veil between Me and your heart, soul, and spirit dissipates. Here, within the flooding light of My presence, you find rest.

You have entered a place where the world can no longer touch you. You have come to Me, your Shelter and your Refuge. You have sought My face and regained your soul. Tarry here for a little while longer. Breathe in My love and peace. Bask in My light. Then go in My strength, sated on Me, the Manna from heaven.

"Behold, I stand at the door [of the church] and continually
knock. If anyone hears My voice and opens the door,
I will come in and eat with him (restore him), and he with Me."
REVELATION 3:20 AMP

This Is the Way

There may be days when you are unsure of the next step on your journey. Let Me be your compass, giving you direction for every path you take.

Know that at any time you can come to Me for renewal, encouragement, strength, fortitude, and guidance. With a sure sense of Me by your side, you will learn how to act instead of react to each and every situation you encounter. With the kingdom of God within you, there is no need to worry about man's kingdom without.

Simply trust, assured that I will not lead you astray. As My Father did with Abraham, I will lead you to a place you may not yet be able to imagine. Yet it is the place I have designated and designed just for you. For there is no one else who can be the person you are, who can do what I have created you to do, who can go where I have called you to go.

From this point on, may your steps be sure. And if by chance any hesitation arises, look to Me. Listen to My soft voice say, "This is the way. Walk in it." Then go forward, knowing I am only a whisper away.

Your ears will hear a word behind you, "This is the way, walk in it," whenever you turn to the right or to the left.
ISAIAH 30:21 AMP

Above All Else

You may be wondering why life can seem so hard sometimes, why you keep falling into the trap of fear, worry, and angst, why the world seems to be so upside down. It is because you are not seeking Me above everything else.

Each morning before your feet hit the floor, spend time with Me. Come into My presence and peace. Allow Me to fill your heart with My love, so much so that it will spill out onto those whose lives you touch.

Determine to view the world through My eyes, to see the light of God in each and every person. Rest in the assurance that all is well. I have laid out a perfect path for you. To find your way, you simply have to stop and ask directions. Be certain that no matter what happens, I am beside you. In My hand is everything you will ever need. Trust. Hope. Relax. Know that I am with you every step of the way.

Above all else in heaven and on earth, seek first My kingdom and My way of doing things, and everything else will fall into place.

"Steep your life in God-reality, God-initiative, God-provisions.
Don't worry about missing out. You'll find all your
everyday human concerns will be met."
MATTHEW 6:33 MSG

Take Heart

There is a time when a woman sees loved ones die, witnesses evil taking the upper hand, and experiences a despair that is almost too much to bear. But take heart. All this is simply an illusion—for I have conquered this world.

Believe that one day you will see your loved ones again. That one day you will see evil put in its place and My goodness reign. Keep your faith that there is reason to hope in this land of the living.

Have a good cry if needed, and then dry your tears. When the grief begins to threaten once more and relief is desperately wanted, simply remind your heart, body, mind, and soul that all is well, that one day you will again see My goodness in this land, and that you need not concern yourself with who, what, when, where, or why. But only come to Me and rest in My presence. Allow Me to fill you with courage and apply a healing balm to your heart. Simply wait, knowing these days of sorrow will pass and that the One who never changes will always be here for you, ready to wipe away your tears, replace your sorrowful sigh with laughter, and turn your grief into joy.

I would have lost heart, unless I had believed that I would see the goodness of the LORD in the land of the living. Wait on the LORD; be of good courage, and He shall strengthen your heart; wait, I say, on the LORD!
PSALM 27:13–14 NKJV

Hidden Reserves

There are some things you find difficult to do in your own strength. So turn to Me. I am here to help you live the life you have been called by our Father to live.

Dig deep into Me. I am your untapped power, your hidden reserves, your infinite supply. There is no need to look any further or to any other source. I hold more power than any food, drug, or superhero. And I hold it all for you.

So do not worry about anything. Just simply tap into Me. Fill yourself with supernatural strength and courage. Know that I am limited by neither time nor space. Thus I can go before you and be with you—all at the same time! And not just this once—but over and over again, and for all time!

I am your help in heaven and on earth. And I'm sticking close to you. Simply open up your heart and soul to My power and your eyes to My presence. Then walk forward—and keep walking. There is nothing to fear, nothing that can get you down when we are together.

*"Be strong and courageous. . . . The L*ORD* himself goes before you and will be with you; he will never leave you nor forsake you. Do not be afraid; do not be discouraged."*
DEUTERONOMY 31:7–8 NIV

In Step with God

My Word is not to be simply glossed over in the morning, a daily chore like making your bed. It is to be read slowly so that its strength and power will permeate your entire being—mind, body, spirit, and soul. This inspired wisdom is to be recalled day and night. Only in this way will it become a natural part of you. Only in this way can your thoughts even begin to parallel the thoughts of Father God.

As the Word becomes a part of you, you will thrive! You will no longer worry or fret but become peaceful of heart and mind. In such a relaxed state, you will make better decisions, knowing that whatever happens in a given situation, all will be well, for you are walking the right way—in step with Me. As you become imbued with wisdom, success shall soon follow. You will be where you were meant to be and get to where you were destined to go.

*"This Book of the Law shall not depart from your mouth,
but you shall read [and meditate on] it day and night,
so that you may be careful to do [everything] in accordance
with all that is written in it; for then you will make your
way prosperous, and then you will be successful."*

Joshua 1:8 amp

Spiritual Eyes

In these moments with Me, gently close your eyes. Envision My presence beside you. Feel My breath upon your face. Bask in the warmth of My light. Your inner eyes are upon Me. Here there is no reason to fear or fret. In your powerlessness, you feel My strength. Breathe easy. Then commit these moments to memory.

In this power, in this memory, reopen your eyes. I am still with you—and always will be no matter what you face today. Don't worry about anything. Simply keep your spiritual eyes on Me. Know that I will never let anything harm you. Know that I will always be with you. Know that you don't have to always have the answer. Look to Me for all wisdom, strength, and power. For all I have is yours. And I have promised I will always be here for you.

Thus, you may this day and all days walk forward in victory, no matter who or what is coming against you. Rest in My might, with your eyes upon Me. For in Me lie all answers.

"For we have no power against this great multitude
that is coming against us; nor do we know
what to do, but our eyes are upon You."
2 CHRONICLES 20:12 NKJV

A Listening Ear

I am ready to speak a good word to you. But sometimes you do not hear. Or you run the other way. Other times you will ask a friend for advice or seek an answer from books. Yet all the while I am vying for your attention.

I, wisdom personified, want to tell you what I am about to do in your life, in your world. Are you listening? Will you be My willing servant?

This relationship we have is not to be one- but two-sided. There is a time for you to speak and then a time for you to listen. And then not just listen, but obey.

I have a word for you, a woman after My own heart. You are also the apple of My eye. I see your face and smile, knowing how stupendous you are, if only you knew it too.

When I come calling your name, open up your ears and heart. Respond with love and obedience. And then, "Behold!" Wondrous things will unfold.

Now the LORD came and stood and called as at other times, "Samuel! Samuel!" And Samuel answered, "Speak, for Your servant hears." Then the LORD said to Samuel: "Behold. . ."
1 SAMUEL 3:10–11 NKJV

Dreams Arise

At night, when there are more shadows than light, worries tend to creep into one's mind. Thought after thought seems to race through your head with no end in sight.

In the midst of your tossing, turn to Me. Remember Me. I am here, My arms stretched out wide, welcoming you to come to Me so that I may enfold you in a loving embrace.

Allow your worries—about the man you love, the children you care for, the friend you would lay down your life for—to fall away. Like an eagle that shelters her eaglets, I will cover you with My feathers. Here you are safe from all harm, all worries, all what-ifs.

I have promised you so much. And these promises are like a solid rock—unchangeable, everlasting, certain, and sure. I will never leave you. You are precious in My sight. Nothing is impossible for you. I bear your burdens—and do so gladly.

Knowing all this, relax. Breathe deep. Trust in Me. I will never let you fall. As the terrors of the night fade away, beautiful dreams arise. Dream of Me. Dream of love. Dream of peace.

He will cover you with his feathers. He will shelter you
with his wings. His faithful promises are your armor and
protection. Do not be afraid of the terrors of the night.
PSALM 91:4–5 NLT

Miracle Maker

Woman, I am ready to do so many miracles in your life. Do you believe Me?

The greater your faith in Me, the more amazing things I can do in your life and in the lives of those around you. Do not limit Me. Train yourself to think outside the box. Humble yourself enough to believe in My grandeur. Push your doubts aside. Remember that I am the One who changed water into wine, healed lepers, calmed the sea and wind, and rose from the dead. There is nothing I *cannot* do—if your faith is big enough.

And once the miracle begins, it will continue for as long as you keep your eyes on Me. So do not look away, or you may sink down into the sea of doubt.

You are a woman of amazing strength. There is no door closed to one who believes in the impossible. And that's My art—to make the impossible possible. Will you help Me? Will you not doubt? Will you believe anything can happen? If so, pray and petition. Watch and wait. Then praise and repeat.

And he did not do many miracles there
because of their lack of faith.
MATTHEW 13:58 NIV

Know Me

I see you as no one else does. Your face, your hands, your size, your shape, your hair, your breath, your sigh—all these I know intimately. To Me, you are no stranger but an extension, an expression of Myself as you move in the light of love, forgiveness, and charity.

Yet at times, it seems I am yet a stranger to you. This will not do.

When you are worshipping or praying to Me, you cannot help but feel My love. Yet when you leave My presence, you sometimes leave Me and My love behind. My light and love are not for you to just experience in a moment of devotions but to carry back out into the world. How else will the world around you be changed?

So, friend and sister, seek Me out daily. Feel the peace of My presence. Bask in the light of My love. Listen to the sound of My breath and My sigh. See Me as you have never seen Me before. Then take Me with you, out into the world. Become an extension of Me. Forgive the seemingly unforgivable. Love the unlovable. Help the helpless.

In doing so, you will begin to know Me as I know you—forever and ever, amen.

"Before I shaped you in the womb, I knew all about you.
Before you saw the light of day, I had holy plans for you."
JEREMIAH 1:5 MSG

Patience

Thousands of earth years ago, an old woman named Sarah chuckled when Father God told her she and her elderly husband, Abraham, would birth a son. When He confronted her about her laughter, she denied mocking Him. But I knew. And so her patience was tested.

As time passed, Sarah became more and more impatient for a son. So she sought to take matters into her own hands and gave her servant Hagar over to Abraham, thinking this was how she, Sarah, would become a mother. Thus was born Ishmael through Hagar and Abraham. And trouble soon followed, first between the women and then between Sarah's promised son, Isaac, and his half brother Ishmael. Had she waited for the promise, much heartache would have been avoided.

Impatience often gives birth to trouble. And it comes about when you see the world through your eyes instead of Mine.

Believe Me when I tell you that I do all things at the perfect time. So rest easy. Do not try to force things to happen, but keep yourself in the flow of the river of life. I am the Living Water, the great Creator. I have you covered in each and every way. So do not go against My current but relax. Breathe. Lean back upon Me.

Your life and hopes are in My good hands. Trust and be satisfied in Me alone, and all your dreams will come true, all your hopes will be realized.

Be still before the Lord; wait patiently
for Him and entrust yourself to Him.
Psalm 37:7 amp

The Source of All

I created woman to be a wonderful, flexible, nurturing vessel for humankind. It is through you that new lives may be created, fed in the womb, and nourished with love and affection that only a mother can give.

Yet you are also a fighter for the ones you love—from your children to your husband.

Yes, I have created you to become many things—a mother, sister, friend, wife, grandmother, coworker, teacher, and more. For you can be anything or anyone you put your mind to, like Deborah of old, who was not only a wife but a prophet, a judge, and a commander of Israel's army. The same love, foretelling, wisdom, and courage that were available to Deborah are available to you. Their source? Me—and Me alone.

So, My sister, come to Me now as the essential you—the daughter of the Lord Almighty. Strip yourself bare of all your varied roles, and focus only on what you as God's daughter need to face this day in strength and victory. This true you, this precious woman, will then receive all the love, foretelling, wisdom, and courage she needs to nurture, lead, and strengthen others in this day. For I, the Source of all you need, will forever fill you up, day by precious day.

Deborah, the wife of Lappidoth, was a prophet
who was judging Israel at that time.
Judges 4:4 nlt

Working Out a Way

I see all. I know exactly what your heart desires. Yet I would have the words of your wants come to Me by your own lips. Tell Me exactly what you want. Show Me exactly what you desire. And I, in return, will answer your prayer in accordance with My wisdom.

You see, I see all things—not just your desires but those of all My other brothers and sisters. Like a child, you may desire something that may not be good for you today, but perhaps it will be tomorrow. So be patient. Continually pare down your focus to what you truly desire with all your mind, body, heart, and soul. And if it would be good for you and the world, your desire shall be granted.

Simply leave all in My hands and go forward, knowing your Father will only give you what is good and right for you in this time and space. And in the meantime, be content, knowing that I am working out a way for you to be all I created you to be—nothing more and nothing less than spectacular today and every day!

Hannah prayed: I'm bursting with GOD-news! I'm walking on air. I'm laughing at my rivals. I'm dancing my salvation. Nothing and no one is holy like GOD, no rock mountain like our God. Don't dare talk pretentiously—not a word of boasting, ever! For GOD knows what's going on. He takes the measure of everything that happens.
1 SAMUEL 2:1–3 MSG

Pure Joy

I am your Rock. Your Fortress. Your solid foundation! Do you see this?

When you come to Me, you seem to know Me. You recognize who I am and what I have done for you. But when you finish your prayers or devotions, you seem to leave Me where I am and try to live life in your own power! This shall not do!

Do you want joy? Do you want peace? Do you want strength? Do you want power? Then, My dear woman, remember that I am always looking out for you! I am always standing by your side! I see what you see—and so much more! So keep Me close. So close that you can hear Me breathe in rhythm with you. So close that you can hear Me whisper. So close that you can feel My power surging through you.

Knowing that I am with you, that I am eager to bless you, and that I am shielding you with all that I am will give you all the joy you could want—so much that it spills over you and onto others who may not yet know Me. With Me truly in your life and the light of your life, your pure joy cannot help but run over!

Light is sown [like seed] for the righteous and illuminates their path, and [irrepressible] joy [is spread] for the upright in heart [who delight in His favor and protection].
PSALM 97:11 AMP

Fallen Burdens

So many people are weighed down by the past. They constantly mull over in their minds, *If only I had done this.* Or *If only I could take that back.* Such thoughts get them nowhere.

Each day is a new day, a new beginning. Forget what happened (or didn't happen) yesterday. Come to Me in this moment. Focus only on Me. There is no use in rehashing the could'ves, would'ves, and should'ves. It's time to reach for the things ahead of you.

That is the ultimate freedom, the path to peace, the road to well-being. Shed that burden that you have been carrying. Let it fall from your shoulders and onto Mine. That is what I came here for. That is the freedom My path allows you. That's what enables you to be an effective worker for Me. For only when the burden has fallen will you be open to receive more and more blessings.

So, woman, forgive all those who have wronged you—including yourself. Let go of all the memories that give you pain. Forget about the what-ifs. Then breathe deeply the air of freedom, the scent of your Christ, who came to free you from every kind of bondage, including burdens that are in reality merely dust.

*One thing I do, forgetting those things which are behind
and reaching forward to those things which are ahead.*
PHILIPPIANS 3:13 NKJV

Streaming Thoughts

You must train yourself, My child, to be a witness to the thoughts that are streaming through your head. The negative thoughts are only shadows of reality, mucking up your mind. Do not let them have sway or power over you. Instead, let them flow through unheeded. Pay no attention to the fear, panic, hatred, lust, grief, and aggression they bring with them. Just allow them to pass away. If more strength is needed, simply call on Me. When you say My name, "Jesus," My light makes all shadows disperse. All evil fades. For it has no strength, no power against Me.

Just keep your mind on Me. Hand over your entire self—mind, body, spirit, soul. I will keep you safe from all harm. I will give you all the joy and strength you need. You need not look anywhere else.

Feed on Me, your Bread of life. Drink of Me, your Living Water. Come to Me, your Burden Bearer, eternal Friend, Light of the world. Rest assured that I will never leave you, fail you, forsake you. And that's the truth. That's My promise and your confidence.

"You will keep in perfect and constant peace the one whose mind is steadfast [that is, committed and focused on You—in both inclination and character], because he trusts and takes refuge in You [with hope and confident expectation]."
Isaiah 26:3 amp

Always Present

You have had your sorrows and temptations in this life, as well as heartbreak, rejection, and derision. And through it all, whether you knew it or not, whether you recognized Me or not, I was walking with you.

In the midst of your fire, I felt the flame. In the midst of your flood, I felt the undercurrent. In the midst of your earthquake, I felt the earth tremble.

No matter where you are, no matter what happens, I am walking this road with you. So stop. Take a rest. Call My name—and then you will see Me. Then you will know that I've been right next to you all along.

Thus there is no reason to dread the fires, floods, or earthquakes in your life. There is no reason to let them shake you up. You can be confident in Me, My presence, My strength. I am holding on to you tightly and will never, ever let you go. Simply put your hand in Mine, and walk on. The Son of God is walking with you.

"Look!" he answered, "I see four men loose, walking in the midst of the fire; and they are not hurt, and the form of the fourth is like the Son of God."

Daniel 3:25 nkjv

Future Plans

You need not worry about anything. Truly, I have it all planned out for you, every aspect of your life. All you need to do is continually tap into Me. Ask Me about each and every move you make. If you feel uncomfortable about something, stop. Have you spoken to Me about it, asked Me if it was a part of the plan for your life?

Whenever you need to make a decision, come to Me first. I will give you the wisdom you need to move forward. Everything I have in mind is for your good. When you make Me—and only Me—your Source, your Hope, your Rock, your Refuge, your Shield, your Strength, your Light, you are on the path to the kingdom of God. And as you walk that road, you are walking with Me. Your future is safe, assured, and perfect. For your future is Me.

So lift yourself above the cares of this world. Gently lay your head upon My shoulder. Rest in My embrace. Feed yourself upon My strength. Know that I will never leave you or forsake you. You need never walk alone.

"I know what I'm doing. I have it all planned out—
plans to take care of you, not abandon you,
plans to give you the future you hope for."
Jeremiah 29:11 msg

Love–Pure and Unfettered

There are some things (and some people) you may never be able to change. But that is not your affair. Your business is loving all—no matter who they are or what they do. For didn't I love you when you were still confused and ignorant of My presence and My ways?

The best way to show others the Way is to shower them with the love you get from Me. That's why I've asked you to feed the hungry, clothe the naked, visit the prisoner. While you are at it, do something nice for the intrusive mother-in-law, the demanding boss, the unfriendly neighbor, the gum-cracking checkout girl, the desperate-looking homeless man. Find a way to reach the heart of others by tapping into My reserves. Each kindness you bestow upon another restores My reserves and comes back at you a hundredfold.

So don't let others irritate. Instead allow them to help you navigate your way through this world. Let them be markers on your road to paradise. Let them see our love for what it is—pure and unfettered.

Who can you bless this way? Who can you love today?

But God showed his great love for us by sending
Christ to die for us while we were still sinners.
ROMANS 5:8 NLT

Lost, Now Found

There is no need for you to hide your face from Me, for I know what you've been doing. I know what you've been going through, how you gave in to temptation, erred in your speech, or made a gross mistake in some other way. And in spite of all the harm you think you've done or the heartache you may have caused yourself or others, know this: I am filled with compassion for you.

For a little while you were lost, but now you are found. You are back in My presence. There may, of course, be some repercussions from your actions, for as you know, you reap what you sow. But also know this—I am celebrating your return, no matter how short or long your absence was! This is because I adore you. Because I do have such great plans for you. Because there is nothing more wonderful than a sheep coming back to the fold.

So do not think I am angry. Do not think I am disgusted with you. Believe Me when I tell you I am overjoyed at your return. And I am thrilled that you are focusing on Me once again.

You have learned a hard lesson. But you have returned to the kingdom of God. I'm so happy you're home. And that is something to celebrate!

"So he returned home to his father. And while he was still a long way off, his father saw him coming. Filled with love and compassion, he ran to his son, embraced him, and kissed him."
Luke 15:20 nlt

The Light

Rest your body. Sit back in your chair. Put your feet flat on the floor. Relax. Allow My light and life to fill you from the top of your head to the bottom of your feet.

Breathe easy. One breath, then two, then three. Let all the troubles of the world fade away. Whatever has happened, has happened. Whatever will be, will be. Let it go. Drift away from the earthly world. Rise up to the kingdom of God.

Come to Me now. In My presence there is peace. Here you are surrounded by a love that can never die. Here there is no sorrow or pain. There is only a light that glows like no other. It is the light of a life with Me.

You too can have this light. It's a light that you can shine into the earthly world. It's a light that will point others to Me. Let this light shine. Let it fill you to overflowing. Let it lead you to all good things.

Rest here for a moment or two longer. Then, as you slowly return to the earthly world, remember the light that you have within. Keep the flame alive by spreading My love. Keep the darkness at bay. Be still. Know that I am God—and that you are the light of this world.

"Be still and know (recognize, understand) that I am God."

Psalm 46:10 amp

The Remedy

Gently, gently lift your head. There is no sorrow so deep that I cannot heal it. No pain so great I cannot remedy it. Come to Me. Put your entire self—not just your mind or just your body, but your mind, body, soul, and spirit—in My hands. Release from yourself any distrust, doubt, and despair as air from a balloon, until there is no debility remaining that would hinder My work, until there is nothing left but a foundation of freedom, a time of rest, and a spark of hope. Then allow Me to build you back up as you abide in Me and My Spirit abides in you. I am your Healer. I am your Remedy. I am the Answer to all your questions. Remain in this secret place with Me. Know that I am the greatest and mightiest force in heaven and on earth. With Me you are vulnerable yet safe; you are home yet a foreigner in a strange place; you are alone yet surrounded by Me and a heavenly host.

But you have come to Mount Zion, to the city of the living God, the heavenly Jerusalem. You have come to thousands upon thousands of angels in joyful assembly. . .You have come to God, the Judge of all. . .to Jesus the mediator of a new covenant.
HEBREWS 12:22–24 NIV

The Journey Ahead

In My strength, you have been victorious. And now you have come off the mountaintop and into this wilderness, exhausted, depressed, and alone. Upon your lips are the words of Elijah: "I've had enough, Lord." You may rest here until you regain your strength and joy.

Upon a touch from My angel, I will awaken you and give you Myself—the Water and Bread of life—for your nourishment. Once you are sated, this spiritual food will give you untold strength so you can continue the work you were designed to do. I will lead you out of this wilderness. I will clear the way ahead. I will give you the next path you are to take. But for now, worry not. Simply know that My angel is watching over you on the first and last steps of each and every path you take, from mountaintop to valley to wilderness to mountaintop again. And know that all the spiritual nourishment you truly need for the journey ahead is found in Me.

Then the angel of the LORD came again and touched him and said, "Get up and eat some more, or the journey ahead will be too much for you." So he got up and ate and drank, and the food gave him enough strength to travel forty days and forty nights.

1 KINGS 19:7–8 NLT

From Dawn to Dusk

Do not be a stranger. As the day breaks, come into My presence. Then linger with Me for a moment. Allow Me to be your morning provision. I am—and have—all you need to face each and every day. If given the opportunity, I will richly nourish your spirit, strengthen your body, spark your mind, and gladden your soul. All this I, the risen Son, will give you before you step one foot on the ground. It is a feast treasured by many saved souls.

So do not bypass these precious moments. Come. Linger. Open yourself to My supply that will fortify you throughout your day.

And then when day is done, the sun has set, come to Me once again. Do not be afraid of the darkness. There is no shadow that can separate us. So lay yourself down. Breathe easy upon your bed. Envision Me beside you once more. Thank Me for the countless blessings you received from My hand. Say a prayer for your family and friends. Then enter the sleep of the innocent. And may your gentle smile be the precursor to the joy of the dreams you are about to witness.

What a beautiful thing, GOD, to give thanks, to sing an anthem to you, the High God! To announce your love each daybreak, sing your faithful presence all through the night.

PSALM 92:1–2 MSG

Dreams

Why do you continue to try to do everything in your own power? Why do you not ask Me for advice, direction, help? You act as if I am to have no part in helping your dreams to come true. Or that you need to carry all the burden of attaining your dream on your own shoulders, as if your strength is the be-all and end-all. Instead of carrying this entire load by yourself, come to Me. Tell Me what your dreams and aspirations are—and why. Lay them in My tender hands. Then rest well in the knowledge that I will enlighten you. That I will give you the wisdom to make the right decisions, to take the right path. I will help you to determine what is best for your life—as well as the people in it. When you bare your heart before Me, when you tell Me everything that is on your mind, when you open up to Me as to no other, I cannot help but be moved. So don't hold back. Tell Me all, and I will help you make all your dreams a reality!

Commit your way to the Lord;
trust in Him also and He will do it.
PSALM 37:5 AMP

Mighty Power

Like Elijah in the cave, you have hidden yourself away, are sleeping in the darkness, and are licking your wounds. What are you doing here? From what are you fleeing? Have people abused you? Has your faith deserted you? Has the dark one convinced you that he is stronger than Father, Son, and Holy Spirit? Have you given up on the world? Are you feeling overwrought, overshadowed, overcome?

Wake up, woman! Have you forgotten that you are the daughter of God the King? That you wear His armor? That you have access to mountain-moving faith? Get back on solid spiritual ground through the Word. Allow the clamor of the world to fall away as you seek Me in prayer. Then, restored and renewed, come out of the shadows and into the pillar of My light. Open your eyes and seek My face. Open your ears and hear My gentle whisper. You have My resurrection power. Thus nothing is impossible for you. You are a child of the light—not a cave dweller!

I also pray that you will understand the incredible greatness of God's power for us who believe him. This is the same mighty power that raised Christ from the dead and seated him in the place of honor at God's right hand in the heavenly realms.
EPHESIANS 1:19–20 NLT

When Tempers Flare

I, your Lord and Master, know the thoughts you think. I know what runs through your head after you've had a heated discussion. But I also know your heart. You are a good woman, mother, worker, sister, daughter, wife, and friend. You have no desire to intentionally hurt anyone or anything. Yet sometimes words seem to fly out of your mouth. And before you know it, they've sparked a firestorm. Sometimes it's not really even the words themselves but the tone of voice, the volume level, or the unable-to-be-hidden intent that comes glaring through. And now you, although you may still be a little angry or upset, are sorry for what you said, for losing your temper. Don't be afraid to confess your feelings to Me or to apologize to the one you think you may have hurt. Although it may be humbling to ask forgiveness, or to even admit that you have done something wrong, you will be filled with so much more joy afterward.

So tell Me all your troubles. Know that I understand. And then go with My strength and blessing to the one your words have hurt. Go in My name, and may My forgiveness and joy go with you, regardless of how your apology is received. For loving others—by word and deed—is always the right thing to do.

"In your anger do not sin": Do not let the sun go down
while you are still angry, and do not give the devil a foothold.
Ephesians 4:26–27 niv

A New Road

Are you ready for a new challenge? Are you following My lead, My promptings, My direction? Do you see the new thing I am leading you to? Too often My sisters miss the open door I have before them. Sometimes it is because they are focused more on the treasures of the earth than the treasures of heaven. Or they are too self-absorbed in their own plans, never looking up to see what I'm doing. But here I am, opening a door for you. There is a new path, a new opportunity for you. Don't miss it!

Forget about the things that happened in the past. This is a new day! It is a new way! Stop for a moment. Look up. Ask Me what I would have you do, where I would have you go. Heed My voice. Listen to My direction. Take off your blinders. Open up your mind and your eyes. Then look around you. There is a new road. Take the first step into the adventure awaiting you. Know that I am with you and will continue to guide you in this new endeavor. Use Me as your GPS—and be amazed at what unfolds!

"Forget about what's happened; don't keep going over old history.
Be alert, be present. I'm about to do something brand-new.
It's bursting out! Don't you see it? There it is! I'm making
a road through the desert, rivers in the badlands."
Isaiah 43:18–19 msg

Listen

You were never meant to walk this road alone. That is one reason I came to earth, to show you the way and to leave you with a Companion, a Comforter, the Holy Spirit. But you also have fellow human travelers, who appear in so many different roles—as mentor, teacher, adviser, friend, husband, brother, sister, mother, father. Each one can teach you in his or her own special way. They are here for you on your journey—and you are here for them on theirs.

So be as gentle with them as you would want them to be with you. Help lift their load—as they help you carry yours. Reach out to them as I reach out to you. Comfort, protect, forgive, inspire, and encourage them—but most of all, pay attention to what they have to say.

One of the greatest ways to show your love is to truly listen to others in your life without judgment or criticism. Simply focus on the part of Me you see in them, and listen as you would have Me listen to you—not letting one precious word drop to the floor unheard.

Live creatively, friends. If someone falls into sin, forgivingly restore him, saving your critical comments for yourself. You might be needing forgiveness before the day's out. Stoop down and reach out to those who are oppressed. Share their burdens, and so complete Christ's law.
GALATIANS 6:1–2 MSG

Dieter's Delight

Don't just rush through your daily devotions. Dig deep down. Be still and silent, and allow My Word to simmer. Make it a part of your daily diet, chewing slowly so you thoroughly digest each and every letter, word, sentence, paragraph, and page. For when you do, those words become a part of your very being, able to be recalled at a moment's notice, saving you from darkness and disaster, lifting you high above earthly troubles, and giving you much-needed strength.

The words of scripture—New and Old—renew, refresh, and re-create you down to the core. They satisfy you like nothing else on this earth. They are to be your food and drink. Your very nourishment. Your manna from heaven. The more those words become a part of your life, the more you know and understand your Lord and Master, and the more I truly become a part of your world. The more time you spend in the Word, the more you will gain delight and joy. Happy and blessed is the woman whose regular diet is soul food.

"When I discovered your words, I devoured them.
They are my joy and my heart's delight."
JEREMIAH 15:16 NLT

First Come, Always Served

Where are you looking for help? To things, other people, money, or institutions? Don't you know that they are all fallible? That none of them are unchangeable, eternal, and filled with the awesome power of God? Do you not know the only thing that can truly save you is Me?

Look to Me—and Me alone—for each and every need! Even though getting you out of the pit *seems* impossible, nothing is too difficult for Me! Can you not wait for Me to rescue you in My own timing? Don't look for other "things" to save you right here and now. Be patient! I have bigger plans in mind for you.

Do you need something to believe in? Don't fall for that false American idol. Look to Me. Do you need or want a man in your life? Don't give yourself to every Tom, Dick, and Harry, but give yourself more fully to Me. Do you need financial help? Come to Me. Have faith that I will provide. Do you need employment? Checking the want ads is fine, but come to Me first. I will open doors you had no clue even existed.

Look to Me before all things, believe in My power—and watch great plans unfold! When you consistently come first to Me, you will always be served!

What sorrow awaits those who look to Egypt for help,
trusting their horses, chariots, and charioteers and
depending on the strength of human armies instead
of looking to the LORD, the Holy One of Israel.
ISAIAH 31:1 NLT

Word Power

So you were going along fine, and then you read something in My Word that has stopped you in your tracks. My daughter, this is a good thing! This Word that you read each and every day is alive! It is speaking directly to your soul! It reaches where nothing else can! It is pointing out something in your life that you need to address. Perhaps there is a friend or neighbor you need to apologize to, a wrong you have been avoiding but need to right. Perhaps there is a child or a younger woman looking for guidance, hope, and direction. Perhaps you have been storing more treasures on earth than in heaven and priorities need to be shifted. Perhaps it is something that goes much deeper, something you cannot quite discern. In each of these cases, there is a reason to praise! I am speaking directly to your life!

I and the Word—one and the same—are indeed alive, leading you, guiding you, helping you. Spend some more time in meditation with Me today. Apply to My wisdom. Ask, seek, knock—then you will know and all things will be set right.

For the word of God is living and active and full of power
[making it operative, energizing, and effective]. It is sharper
than any two-edged sword, penetrating as far as the division
of the soul and spirit [the completeness of a person], and of
both joints and marrow [the deepest parts of our
nature], exposing and judging the very thoughts
and intentions of the heart.
HEBREWS 4:12 AMP

Overflowing Blessings

You are like every good woman, oftentimes driven to nurture and care for others before nurturing or caring for yourself. Yet living thus may weaken you, not only physically, mentally, and emotionally, but spiritually as well. Take this moment to reevaluate your life. Come before Me and be totally honest. Where are you giving most of yourself—to your job, your family, your husband, your friends, your education, your church? If so, stop. Reconsider.

Give your all first to Me, your Lord and Savior. Bring all your tithes—your talents, hopes, dreams, love, passion, gifts, mind, soul, spirit—to Me. Put them in My possession. Trust Me with all that you are, have, and ever hope to be. Then see what happens!

Watch how the windows of heaven will open and pour blessing upon blessing into your life. Let go of all you are holding on to—doubts, worries, fears, possessions, money, jealousies, nightmares, anger, confusion, fear, memories, grief, stress, feelings of unworthiness—so that you can open up your hands to capture all the gifts I am bursting to give you. Give to Me until I overflow onto you.

"Bring all the tithes (the tenth) into the storehouse, so that
there may be food in My house, and test Me now in this,"
says the Lord of hosts, "if I will not open for you the windows
of heaven and pour out for you [so great] a blessing
until there is no more room to receive it."
MALACHI 3:10 AMP

Time of Testing

When you go through a time of testing, do not despair. There will be better days ahead. For now, simply know that I am with you every step of the way. If you cannot get over, under, or around an obstacle, I will help you get through it. All I require of you is faith.

Believe that I am holding your hand, that I have a firm grip on you and will never let you go. When darkness comes and panic begins to set in, feel My tug and allow your heart to calm. Know that everything will turn out all right, that through this testing, you are growing and learning. Once you are out on the other side, you will know the landscape of this particular trial so well that you will be able to help others through it. So don't worry about the what-ifs. Don't speculate on what might've been. Simply take deep breaths. Remember the times I have gotten you through in the past. Keep in mind all the things I did to save you—and know that I am not about to let go of you now. Be firm in these thoughts. And you will feel My peace break through, from My Spirit to yours.

"For I am the LORD your God who takes hold of your right hand and says to you, Do not fear; I will help you. Do not be afraid."
ISAIAH 41:13–14 NIV

A Stretch of Faith

I, Jesus Christ, can do anything, for I am God's one and only Son. So why is it that, at times, you limit Me? If only you had the faith of the commander I met thousands of years ago. He desired healing for his servant boy. That in itself is commendable, that this centurion would come and chase Me down for a blessing for a young servant. But what was even more commendable was that he said all I had to do was say the word—and he knew the boy would be cured!

Do you have that faith? Do you trust that all I have to do is say the word and what you believe will be done—in the twinkling of an eye? When I was walking among you, God in the form of flesh, I healed many, many people of illness. I walked on water. I calmed the sea and the wind. I turned water into wine. I made the blind to see, the lame to walk. I withered a fig tree with mere words. When My disciples saw it, they marveled. And My words to them are the same words I am now saying to you: "Have a constant faith in God. And whatever you believe will take place will be done." The same goes for you, woman. Constantly be stretching your faith, and watch amazing things unfold.

Then Jesus said to the centurion, "Go! Let it be done just as you believed it would." And his servant was healed at that moment.
MATTHEW 8:13 NIV

Divine Inspiration

There are so many things you probably don't understand about God the Father, the Holy Spirit, and Me. And yet you really don't need to understand all to believe. All you really need to know is that I make the invisible visible. That the eagle climbs at My command. The seasons change at My calling. As winter approaches, I send some birds south. Through My power, the earth, moon, sun, and stars maintain their orbits. I know and understand this world, from the depths of the earth to the farthest reaches in the sky. I know each forest, pasture, mountain, valley, city, town, oasis, and desert. I know down to the last atom every living thing I have created—including you. There is nothing you can hide from Me. There is no question that I cannot answer.

All I ask of you is to have faith in Me. To understand that when I speak, things happen. To believe that everything I create and have created has its purpose. Yours is to worship Me. To love Me with all your heart, soul, strength, and mind. To love others as you love yourself. Begin to live your purpose. Let nothing stand in your way. Simply look to Me. Seek My face. Love—and be loved. Follow in My footsteps. Become My divine inspiration.

By faith [that is, with an inherent trust and enduring confidence in the power, wisdom and goodness of God] we understand that the worlds (universe, ages) were framed and created [formed, put in order, and equipped for their intended purpose] by the word of God, so that what is seen was not made out of things which are visible.
HEBREWS 11:3 AMP

A Praiseworthy Mind-Set

Feeling stuck? If so, your head is too much in this world and not enough in Mine. Lift yourself out of the darkness and into the light of My Word. Consider those women who have gone before, the heroes of old—Miriam, Deborah, Rahab, Esther, Abigail, Naomi, and Ruth. And the heroes of new—Elizabeth, Mary, Mary Magdalene, Joanna, Lydia, and Lois. Remember their faith, commitment, strength, perseverance, courage, and confidence.

Look away from the flood. Seek the rainbow. Keep your mind off the sinners, and focus on the saints. Do not allow yourself to be swallowed by the shadows of this earth. But strain your ears to hear a good word—and may your mouth be eager to give a good word back. Do not become bowed down by the burdens of the world. Instead, allow them to slip off your back as you rise up to the ways of love and the Lord. Stay in tune with the heavenly harmonies of Father God, and you will be in sync with His angels.

Friends, I'd say you'll do best by filling your minds and meditating on things true, noble, reputable, authentic, compelling, gracious—the best, not the worst; the beautiful, not the ugly; things to praise, not things to curse. Put into practice what you learned from me, what you heard and saw and realized. Do that, and God, who makes everything work together, will work you into his most excellent harmonies.

<small>Philippians 4:8–9 msg</small>

Refuge

When you are sore and weary, run to Me. When you are tired of your frantic pace, run to Me. When you are frightened, confused, and overwhelmed by the darkness of this world, run to Me. When you can no longer read My Word through your tears, run to Me. When you feel that all is lost and you can no longer go on, run to Me—for I am.

I am all the nourishment you need, for I am your Living Water and miraculous Manna. I am all the protection you need, for I am your breastplate. I am all the comfort you could want, for no shoulder is bigger than Mine. I, your Strong Tower, am your Shelter in the mightiest of storms. Here in My presence, no evil can touch you. Nothing can penetrate My shield of love for the people who are called by My name.

So in your time of trial, turn to no one but Me. And you will rest secure in My everlasting arm that is never too short to pull you out of danger and into My protective hold. Come. Abide in Me as I abide in My Father. Here you may rest. Here you will come to no harm. Here you shall remain until you have been restored and are ready to go on.

The name of the LORD is a strong tower; the righteous
runs to it and is safe and set on high [far above evil].
PROVERBS 18:10 AMP

Banked Promises

Has My Word fallen on deaf ears, distracted minds, drained hearts, defiant souls, and diverted spirits? If so, how will you be able to defend yourself from malicious slander, worldly "wisdom," misdirected love, and societal evil? I implore you, daughter of God, to take the Word deep into your very being. Open your ears to hear each nuance, to understand each intention of the Holy Spirit who strives to communicate, to make everything clear to you. Focus your mind by memorizing those verses that have truly reached your soul. Allow them to become a part of your being, to penetrate to the heart of your matter, and so fill it with life-giving power and love. Open up your soul to the absolute truth and wisdom of Me so that I truly become your one and only Lord and Savior.

This is how you will find yourself unable to be touched or tempted by evil, how you will become wise in all ways of living and be seen as one of God's own. And in these ways attract others to the God who fills your entire being, giving your open ears a good word, your focused mind food for thought, your empty heart overflowing love, your soul the blessings that come with obedience, and your spirit the joy of abiding and joining with Me.

I've banked your promises in the vault of my heart so I won't sin myself bankrupt. Be blessed, GOD; train me in your ways of wise living. I'll transfer to my lips all the counsel that comes from your mouth.

PSALM 119:11–13 MSG

Food for Thought

Thoughts are very powerful things, for from them material things are birthed. So, dear sister, about what are you thinking?

Consider Job. He fed his thoughts on his fears—and what he feared ended up coming upon him. Some people feed on worries—and those worries come upon them. Some feed on sickness—and catch every illness that can be caught. When you get it into your mind that you're going to have a bad day, chances are you are calling a bad day into being. But this should not be so! You have at your fingertips an amazing resource to keep your troubles at bay. It is My Word.

Fill your mind with reassurances of My love. See yourself protected in My arms. Sing My psalms, and rise up in faith. Follow the proverbs, and walk forward in wisdom. Make the words of My Sermon on the Mount part of your life and that life will be blessed. Consistently read, believe, think about, and walk in My words, and birth a world of beauty, light, and abundance.

"For the thing which I greatly fear comes upon me, and that of which I am afraid has come upon me. I am not at ease, nor am I quiet, and I am not at rest, and yet trouble still comes [upon me]."
JOB 3:25–26 AMP

Spiritual Seeds

Every farmer knows that whatever he plants, that is what he will reap. If he plants seeds of wheat, he will harvest wheat. If he plants corn, he will harvest corn. It also follows that the more seed a farmer sows, the bigger his crop. These are both physical laws. But they are also a reflection of spiritual laws. If you sow seeds of discord, that is what you will reap. It is the same with seeds of discontent, dishonor, and disappointment. Once a seed is sown, it cannot help but be reaped. And the more of something you sow, the more of that you will harvest.

So I ask you, dear sister, what are you planting in your life? What crops are coming up for you—and in what amount? Know that you cannot fool God. He sees, feels, and hears what you are planting—and He is giving you the same in return. So dig deep into the Word. Meditate on its meaning. Then, with the help of the Holy Spirit, plant spiritual seeds of love, joy, peace, and patience in your life. Add kindness, goodness, and faithfulness. Make room for gentleness and self-control. And come harvesttime, you will find spiritual fruit that you—and those around you—can grow on!

Do not be deceived: God cannot be mocked. A man reaps what he sows. Whoever sows to please their flesh, from the flesh will reap destruction; whoever sows to please the Spirit, from the Spirit will reap eternal life.

Galatians 6:7–8 niv

The Wisdom of God

Do not lose hope and faith if you are mocked or called foolish because of your belief in Me and My Word. Even My disciples had trouble totally understanding what I was doing while on earth. When told I had risen again, the Eleven thought the words of the women were nonsense. But that did not take away the power and effect of the truth of the matter. And I am the Way, the Truth, and the Life. All of My Word reveals the power of God. It brings to light His wisdom—even though it seems like foolishness to the world of men.

Know that even if your mind cannot understand the who, what, when, where, why, and how of the Gospel and all that preceded it, it matters not. For God, through Me and My Word, has saved, is saving, and will save all who believe in Me. He has made you His daughter through faith in Me. What else is there to know? Simply believe in the Word. Believe in its power. And as you continue to walk with God, Me, and the Holy Spirit, your life will, in the eyes of this foolish world, become an extraordinary example of the supernatural power of God.

To those whom God has called, both Jews and Greeks, Christ the power of God and the wisdom of God. For the foolishness of God is wiser than human wisdom, and the weakness of God is stronger than human strength.
1 Corinthians 1:24–25 niv

Blaze of Praise

Your prayers are what give our Father God an opening to work His way in your life. The energy you send up to Him and the passion you display show Him how urgent each of your requests for His intercession are. Your words need not be perfect. Your meaning need not be totally clear. God knows what you need before you ask Him. He understands how you are feeling—and why. He longingly and lovingly wants to have a relationship with you, and prayer is the wonderful way of communicating with Him.

So go to your secret place. In that refuge, quiet your mind, heart, spirit, and soul. Then begin with identifying—for God and yourself—the amazing and absolute holiness of the One to whom you are praying. Follow with words asking Him to reveal Himself and His ways in your life. Tell Him that you are prepared and want Him to do things here on earth as they are in heaven. Acknowledge that from His hand and His alone you receive your sustenance. That you are ready—and willing—to forgive others as He has forgiven you. Request that He keep you from the devil's wiles and ways. And, in a blaze of praise, acknowledge that He, God, is the Supreme Being, with all the power, beauty, glory, and honor in His name. So be it! So be you with God!

"In this manner, therefore, pray:
Our Father in heaven, hallowed be Your name."
MATTHEW 6:9 NKJV

Open Eyes

You are in dire straits. And before you know it, your vision seems unclear. In your panic, your mind betrays you. You are no longer sure of the invisible power, so much are your eyes filled with earthly circumstances and apprehensions. When you are in such a state, I am here to tell you there is nothing to fear. What you see is not the be-all and end-all. There is more to the invisible and spiritual world than you could ever know in your earthly form. Be not afraid. The powers that are with you are so much more than what appears to be coming against you.

Go back to what you know of our Father, Me, and the Spirit. We have overcome all. We are with you, surrounding you. Open up the eyes of your heart and your spirit—and see the truth of the matter! Behold your Father God who can divide the seas and rivers, blind an entire army, and stop the sun and the moon. Behold your Brother Jesus who can raise the dead, heal the leper, calm the wind, and silence the sea. Behold the Holy Spirit who gifts prophets, priests, laypeople, and kings. Open your eyes and see the power of God surrounding you—within and without. Believe—and you will be saved!

"Do not fear, for those who are with us are more than those who are with them." And Elisha prayed, and said, "Lord, I pray, open his eyes that he may see." Then the Lord opened the eyes of the young man, and he saw. . . The mountain was full of horses and chariots of fire.
2 Kings 6:16–17 nkjv

Standing Still

Someone you love has encountered a situation, a problem, an obstacle. You are not sure how to advise this person. All you can do is feel his or her pain, anguish, and fear. At first, you rack your brain trying to figure out a solution, but you are too close to the person and the issue. Your heart is in your throat, and you don't know where to turn. Then, having exhausted all your human efforts and still knowing no way to fix things and having no peace, you come to Me. You realize this is too much for you to bear. You find yourself on your knees, admitting that I am the only One who can help you and your loved one.

My ears ring with joy at your pleas—not because you are under duress but because you realized you needed to come to Me! I already know the situation but now know the degree to which you are making yourself available to receive My wisdom, hope, and comfort. As you unburden your heart and I take things on My own shoulders, you rise. All you need to do now is follow My direction, walk in My wisdom, and breathe in My peace. The fight is now Mine—and Mine alone. Your job? To stand still and witness the victory I will set before you.

"You will not even need to fight. Take your positions;
then stand still and watch the LORD's victory. He is
with you. . .do not be afraid or discouraged."
2 CHRONICLES 20:17 NLT

Think, Then Speak

As a mother, sister, daughter, friend, wife, mother-in-law, co-worker, aunt, or daughter-in-law, your life and words touch the hearts of many, including your own. The things you say aloud to others and yourself—even in jest—can have a lifelong effect on the hearers. That is why it is so important to think before you speak. To make sure your words are encouraging, true, praise-worthy, necessary, gentle, kind, and uplifting.

There is so much darkness in the world. Use your words—written and spoken—to build others up, not tear them down. If you are not sure what to say, say nothing. If you feel My prompting, pray for wisdom before you speak. In all situations, know this: the words that come out of your mouth will be a reflection of the influence your knowledge of Me has had on your life.

But no one can tame the tongue. It is restless and evil, full of deadly poison. Sometimes it praises our Lord and Father, and sometimes it curses those who have been made in the image of God. And so blessing and cursing come pouring out of the same mouth. Surely, my brothers and sisters, this is not right!
JAMES 3:8–10 NLT

Quietness and Confidence

How many times will you seek to do things in your own power before coming to Me for help? How often will you find yourself stressed out because you've forgotten where your true strength comes from? Yes, you are human. But you also have the light of God within you. You need to feed that fire by spending time with Me and in My Word. So stop running hither and yon, looking for answers, joy, and purpose in earthly wisdom and material possessions. Take a few moments to rest in Me, to be recharged in My power, to regain your strength.

Only I can give you the peace you need. Only I can calm your heart within so you can face the world without. Only I can give you the confidence to accomplish all you have been created to do. Only I can give you the wisdom to live a heavenly life on earth. So slow your steps. Remember and revel in your complete dependence upon Me. Then, and only then, will true joy fill your heart and the flame of your spirit light up the darkness in this world.

For the Lord GOD, the Holy One of Israel has said this,
"In returning [to Me] and rest you shall be saved,
in quietness and confident trust is your strength."
ISAIAH 30:15 AMP

Safety Net

I alone am the answer to your worries. I alone can give you true peace. When you are fraught with worries, come into My presence. Speak My healing words to soothe your heart and spirit. Continually repeat, "Jesus is with me. All is well."

I can help you—and your loved ones—in any situation. I can not only save you spiritually but keep you safe physically. You need run to no other place but My arms. I am your Shepherd, willing to carry you, to die for you, to lead you, to heal you. I stand between you and the evil, the wolves of this world. With My staff and My rod ready to guide and protect you, you can rest easy. This peace, this confidence that only I can give you cannot be bought. It is fully and freely given—from My heart to yours, from My Spirit to yours, from My mind to yours, from My soul to yours. Expect nothing less in the hours between sunset and sunrise. Bask in My peace. Slumber in My presence. Take that great leap of faith, for I am your safety net, on earth and in heaven.

In peace [and with a tranquil heart] I will both
lie down and sleep, for You alone, O LORD,
make me dwell in safety and confident trust.

PSALM 4:8 AMP

Rock of Ages

You have run to a house of straw to save you when you could've had help from Me—the Rock of Ages. I have helped you out so many times before. What took you so long in coming to Me now? Had the world convinced you that you could only solve this problem with earthly logic? Woman—say it isn't so!

Remember that My eye is always on you. My truth is at your fingertips. My Word is already on your tongue—and written on your heart.

The world has got everything upside down! It is My wisdom—not man's—that can make the impossible possible. It is My arm that is never too short to pull you up out of a pit. It is My solution that is far above any thoughts or imaginings of humankind. Commit your ways and means to My hands alone. Make Me your primary aid—and you will be on the winning side.

"You asked God for help and he gave you the victory. God is always on the alert, constantly on the lookout for people who are totally committed to him. You were foolish to go for human help when you could have had God's help. Now you're in trouble."
2 Chronicles 16:8–9 msg

Spirit of Power

This world would have you be afraid of your own shadow. Fortunately, you are My sister. And as such, you understand that God has given you the courage and boldness you need to live the life you were born to live. So do not give in to the fear of growing old and of not having enough.

Do not cringe when the world tells you that you are not living up to its standards of beauty, poise, and wealth. Simply smile and walk away from the temptation to believe the world's lies.

You are a daughter of God. He knows how many hairs are on your head. He cares about every breath you take and every vow you make. And I, your Brother, value you so much that I sacrificed My life to save yours. And now I am living inside of you, leading you in the way you are to go, giving you the resurrection power to do all that you are designed to do.

So do not shy away from the challenge. Instead, embrace it. And let God's awesome power lead you to be the best you were made to be.

For God did not give us a spirit of timidity or cowardice or fear,
but [He has given us a spirit] of power and of love and of sound
judgment and personal discipline [abilities that result
in a calm, well-balanced mind and self-control].

2 Timothy 1:7 amp

Sweet Forgiveness

What is wonderful and humbling about forgiveness is not just giving it—but asking for it. When you come to Me, your heart in your hand, asking My forgiveness, it touches My heart, deep down. For in this desire for forgiveness, in this act of humility, you are closest to My Father's Spirit.

It is the same feeling that a mother gets when her child humbly comes into her presence, eyes down on the ground, feet shuffling, and tells her he broke her favorite china cup. Her tears cannot help but well up in her eyes as the mother sees the sincere remorsefulness and sorrow in her son's face. And as the years pass, wouldn't it be a wonderful lesson for him if she herself humbly asks him for forgiveness when she does him a wrong?

Forgiveness is sweet. And if it can be granted by our Father to you all the years of your life, you shall be able to grant it to all those who wrong you—even if it takes 490 times.

Then Peter came to Him and said, "Lord, how often shall my brother sin against me, and I forgive him? Up to seven times?" Jesus said to him, "I do not say to you, up to seven times, but up to seventy times seven."
MATTHEW 18:21–22 NKJV

Like a Child

Where is the joyful innocence you once had? Where have the easy spirit, the trusting nature, the curious mind, the happy exuberance, and the enthusiasm gone? Do not let this world's shadows overcome your light. Do not let its wisdom drown out your spiritual intuition and discernment. Do not let its dog-eat-dog and it's all-about-me attitude sweep you up in its embrace.

Instead, go against the worldly current by riding in the boat with Me. There will be times of storm, when the winds and the waves threaten to capsize your vessel. But with Me in the boat, you will never sink down into the depths but will walk on the water and someday rise up to paradise to be with Me. Heaven is the only true kingdom to aspire to, for it will still be there when all the earthly kingdoms fall away.

So live this life with Me in joy! Trust and keep on trusting. Forgive and be forgiven. Love and be loved. Laugh, love, leap—and sing to the Lord a new song, the one you've kept hidden in your childlike heart.

[Jesus] said, "I assure you and most solemnly say to you, unless you repent [that is, change your inner self—your old way of thinking, live changed lives] and become like children [trusting, humble, and forgiving], you will never enter the kingdom of heaven. Therefore, whoever humbles himself like this child is greatest in the kingdom of heaven."
MATTHEW 18:3–4 AMP

Right Paths

How much do you trust Me? With your life—or just your soul?

I trusted you with My entire being. I saved you even before you were formed in the womb. So why not trust Me now? If you have a decision to make or a problem that needs solving, My ears are ready and willing to hear all about it. There is no need for you to try to go it alone. Simply come to Me, and trust Me with all your heart—and mind!

As the Son of God, I have so much more wisdom that you can tap into—at any time and in any place. I am only a whisper of a prayer away. "Jesus, help!" is a prayer I constantly answer for those I love. So come to Me. Seek My wisdom. Listen for My voice in every situation you encounter. Recognize Me for who I am. And I will not fail to keep you on the right path and walking forward in supernatural confidence.

*Trust in and rely confidently on the LORD with all your heart
and do not rely on your own insight or understanding. In all
your ways know and acknowledge and recognize Him,
and He will make your paths straight and smooth
[removing obstacles that block your way].*

PROVERBS 3:5–6 AMP

A Woman Aglow

The world you live in seems to be growing somewhat darker. But that need not be any concern of yours. For the darker the world—the longer its shadows—the brighter My light becomes in you.

So do not abide in the shadows of this world. Do not conform to the image of today's woman. You are a daughter of the King. You already outshine all the jewels on earth. Your heart and mind are aglow with the wisdom and knowledge of the God who resides within you. You do not need the trappings of this world to emit your beauty. So keep your mind transformed and renewed each and every day by keeping close to Me and My Word. If you feel yourself slipping under the shadow, enticed by the trappings of the world, dragged down to its level, simply remind yourself, "My mind is on God alone. He is all I need." In so doing, you will not only become all He has purposed you to be—but become the *best* you can be.

And do not be conformed to this world [any longer with its superficial values and customs], but be transformed and progressively changed [as you mature spiritually] by the renewing of your mind [focusing on godly values and ethical attitudes], so that you may prove [for yourselves] what the will of God is, that which is good and acceptable and perfect [in His plan and purpose for you].
ROMANS 12:2 AMP

A New Challenge

You are ready for a new challenge but unsure about your next step. Take your time. Look for My direction. Listen for My voice. You have stepped out before—and can do it again. Simply remember that each transition is a new beginning. That there is nothing you need to be afraid of when you are walking in the path I have laid out for you.

If there is ever any doubt, seek Me in prayer. Know that I am with you every step of the way. If you stumble, I will quickly grab your hand and balance you so that you can regain your foothold. Continually rise to new challenges. Stretch yourself so that you can become all God has created you to be. Never doubt your footing. Never fear humankind. After all—you're in My hands. Nothing can truly harm you. Then, when you arrive at your new destination, learn all that you can. Be My light in that corner of the world by loving all you meet. Become an expression of Me, an extension of My compassion. Spread the Word and change the world.

Stalwart walks in step with GOD; his path blazed by GOD,
he's happy. If he stumbles, he's not down for
long; GOD has a grip on his hand.
PSALM 37:23–24 MSG

Seek the Lord

Why do you continue to attempt things in your own power? Why do you not reach out to and rely on Father God in every aspect of your life? It's not that you should not seek out physicians to aid in healing your body. Nor should you not seek out advice from pastors, friends, family members, fellow believers, coworkers, or spouses. There are many who have the gift of healing, wisdom, helps, prophecy, discernment—and more! But they are merely mortal. They are not the best and last authority on any matter. They are not the God of all creation who knows every thought, feeling, and facet of your personality. They cannot divine what is truly in your soul or what path God has laid out for you. There is only one way to find the true power and path. And that is to come to Me. I will bring you to the Father. I will clear the obstacles out of your way. Seek the Lord your God; rely on Him alone. He will make all your paths straight. He will heal you—body, spirit, and soul.

In the thirty-ninth year of his reign Asa developed a disease in his feet. His disease was severe, yet even in his illness he did not seek the Lord, but [relied only on] the physicians.
2 Chronicles 16:12 amp

Re-creation Powers

When I was put in the tomb, My followers thought that was the end. But it was just the beginning! By the power of God, I was restored to life—and what a life! In this new body, I could walk through walls and appear seemingly out of nowhere! Those who were not sure of My resurrection and restorative powers could actually physically touch Me—and be truly and totally convinced that it was Me and that I had, indeed, risen from the dead.

My death, which seemed to make things appear so hopeless, gives you the best chance for your own re-creation. Know that God has a plan for you. Understand that He is determined to make you what you were designed to be. He has a vision for your life that cannot be deterred or obscured. Through each and every experience you are being re-created and strengthened until you become the ultimate you.

After you have suffered for a little while, the God of all grace [who imparts His blessing and favor], who called you to His own eternal glory in Christ, will Himself complete, confirm, strengthen, and establish you [making you what you ought to be].

1 PETER 5:10 AMP

Humbly at Peace

To become all that God has designed you to be, you must not let pride come between you and Him. For when you do, when you puff yourself up, you become more in love with the vision of who you think you are than the vision of who God may want you to be.

So be modest in every aspect of your life; after all, it is God who has created your mind, body, spirit, and soul. Your intelligence, appearance, heart, and personality were all formed by Him—with no help from you. Allow Him to have full control. Fill your mind with His Word. Treat your body as His temple. Align your spirit and soul under His direction. And when the moment is right, He will promote you to a seat of honor. Meanwhile, allow no bad news or concerns to disturb the peace you find in Him. Take all your focus off what has or has not happened and put it on what God has been doing and will continue to do through you to make this world a better place—for you and all the women to follow your path.

So humble yourselves under the mighty power of God,
and at the right time he will lift you up in honor. Give all your
worries and cares to God, for he cares about you.
1 Peter 5:6–7 nlt

Eyes Open

While God is working out His renovation of you, be sure to keep strong in your faith. Keep your eyes open to any snares set up by the evil one. He may tempt you into believing that God has had no hand in your life. You have gotten where you are because of your own intelligence, looks, ability, personality, and spirit. Although it is fair to say that you have had some hand in your development, it's only because of your obedience to God, your belief in Me, and the help of the Holy Spirit that you are who you are and where you are today.

Because of your humble attitude, God has given you all the love and the grace you need to become the woman you are destined to be. So, as with all My other brothers and sisters—some who have suffered more, some who have suffered less than you yourself—know that you are not in this alone. You have fellow sojourners who have been called to embark upon the same journey with the ultimate goal of sharing in the eternal glory through Me, your Christ.

Stay alert! Watch out for your great enemy, the devil.
He prowls around like a roaring lion, looking for someone
to devour. Stand firm against him, and be strong in your faith.
Remember that your family of believers all over the world
is going through the same kind of suffering you are.
1 Peter 5:8–9 nlt

Power of Intentions

Intentions are very powerful things. When you set an intention and then act upon it, amazing things happen. But even more amazing is that Father God can take whatever intention you have and make it work according to His plan—not only for you but for everyone else in your world. You see, *He* is the one with the ultimate power.

So no matter what comes against you, employ the power of rejoicing, of praising, of giving all cares up to God. Disregard whatever bad intentions others may have against you—their curses, their discouragements, their insults. Allow disparagements to simply roll off your back. Such things will harm the wrongdoers so much more than they will ever harm you—if ever! Instead, all those things will work together not only to accomplish God's will to help others, but to lift you to a higher, loftier place. And in that place, you can't help but be fearless, understanding, calm, forgiving, and totally content. After all, it's up to God to avenge any wrongs. You are simply here as an instrument of His good hand.

But Joseph said to them, "Don't be afraid. Am I in the place of God? You intended to harm me, but God intended it for good to accomplish what is now being done, the saving of many lives. So then, don't be afraid. I will provide for you and your children."
GENESIS 50:19–21 NIV

God Only Knows

Why must you strain yourself, racking your brain, trying to figure out all the whys of life? Instead, rest in the knowledge that there are some things that only Father God knows. He has the entire plan in His hands. He is working things out for the good of one and all. He, through Me, is calling all believers to a trusting faith—to a place of peace within them. It is He who will make the dead to rise again upon My return. He is working His way through every detail, through the works of every being.

So rest easy. Be assured that God has all the answers, which are good and true. You need only respond to His call, to join Him in this great work. You need only follow the great commandments—to love God with all your heart, soul, strength, and mind. And to love others as you love yourself. So relax. Rest. Trust. Be at peace within and without. And most of all, love everyone—rich and poor, young and old, kind and cruel, ruler and laborer, believer and nonbeliever, giver and taker. And leave the rest to God, who knows all.

GOD's Spirit took me up and set me down in the middle of an
open plain strewn with bones. . . . He said to me, "Son of man,
can these bones live?" I said, "Master GOD, only you know that."
EZEKIEL 37:1, 3 MSG

No More Fetters

You are a woman with amazing opportunities. When you take your eyes off the ground and look up with a God perspective, there is nothing you cannot do. Hope in God. Wait for His timing. Expect good things to happen. Instead of seeing yourself as a limited being, cut away the fetters of your mind. Break the chain that binds you to self-limiting beliefs.

You have My resurrection power. You have God's strength and protection. You have the Holy Spirit's wisdom and direction. Soar as you were divinely designed to do. Rise above pride, pettiness, selfishness, self-absorption, greed, narrow-mindedness, and fear. Break away from the comfort of the ordinary and seek out a new world, the one God is calling you to. And as you rise, as you mount up to the sun, you will find God becoming clearer and clearer. In His strength, you will not grow tired but find each updraft taking you higher and higher into His will. Wait. Expect. Change. And mount up. In His power, you will soar.

But those who wait for the LORD [who expect, look for, and hope in Him] will gain new strength and renew their power; they will lift up their wings [and rise up close to God] like eagles [rising toward the sun]; they will run and not become weary, they will walk and not grow tired.

ISAIAH 40:31 AMP

Your Remedy

You are in despair. Uncertain of ever finding a remedy for your pain. You have exhausted all your earthly resources—but you have never exhausted Me. Helpless, feeling lost in the crowd, you may have given up hope. But you have forgotten to trust in Me. Then one day, you quietly separate from the mass of bodies around you. As you emerge from the shadows, an eternal light breaks through to your thoughts. With a sudden revelation, you say to yourself, *There is one last chance for me. Perhaps—no, not perhaps! Something is telling me that, yes, He can save me! He is my remedy.* Quietly, almost fearfully, you come up behind Me and touch the fringe of My robe. I can feel the virtue, the power, the healing energy going out of Me and into you. In that instant, in that quiet space of light, in that eternal moment, you are healed. What took you so long?

> *"Daughter, your faith [your personal trust and confidence in Me] has restored you to health; go in peace and be [permanently] healed from your suffering."*
> MARK 5:34 AMP

Amazing Praise

When you face trouble, praise. When you are filled with fear, praise. When you are threatened and are uncertain of what to do, praise. When you need help from Me and My Father, praise. When you are discouraged, praise. When you meet the enemy face-to-face, praise. Lift up your head, seek My face, look for My light, then praise My name in a very loud voice: "Give thanks to the Lord! His amazing love lasts forever! He is the First and the Last! He is unchangeable! He is undefeatable! With Him in my life, no man or woman can harm me."

With such a mind-set, such a statement emanating from your lips, you will have victory—such victory that you will not be able to carry all the blessings you gain at My hand. Such amazing praise, such a firm assurance in Me and My promises, cannot help but result in triumph!

As they began to sing and praise, the LORD set ambushes against the men of Ammon and Moab and Mount Seir who were invading Judah, and they were defeated. . . . So Jehoshaphat and his men went to carry off their plunder, and they found among them a great amount of equipment and clothing and also articles of value—more than they could take away.
2 CHRONICLES 20:22, 25 NIV

Continual Renewal

Why are you down in the mouth? Look up! Bless Father God. He always has good in mind for you. Since the day you were separated from Him in Eden, He has worked to bring you closer and closer to Himself. For thousands of years, He has given His people victory. He has saved them from themselves. He has conquered armies, He has forgiven gross transgressions against Him, He has pardoned the seemingly unpardonable, and He has kept His promises. He even sacrificed Me so you could reside with Him forever.

So don't forget all God has done for you—and all He has planned for you. He will continually fill your life with good things—from the cradle to the grave. It's not an age thing—it's a God thing. He will continually be renewing your heart, soul, body, spirit, and mind. Do not worry about what the flesh looks like. Focus on continuing to grow your spirit more and more into the likeness of Me, His precious Son. Come with Me and feel His power, His strength, His replenishing Spirit. Daughter of God, continue to rise up and meet Him with praise!

Bless and affectionately praise the LORD, O my soul, and do not forget any of His benefits. . . . Who satisfies your years with good things, so that your youth is renewed like the [soaring] eagle.

PSALM 103:2, 5 AMP

The Crazy Law of Love

Love is the spirit of all the laws of God. It is what He wants from you above all things. Love is a reflection of God—because God is love. Love is the reason I laid down My life for you. And it's what God wants in return. And not just a superficial love. God wants you to love Him with every breath of your being. He wants you to love Him with not just a small or single part of you—but with *all* your heart, *all* your soul, and *all* your mind. And not just a sometime love—but an all-day, everyday love—with no holds barred! That's the first part.

The second part goes along with it. God wants you to love all others as you love yourself. That means respecting yourself. Looking out for the good of your own soul—as well as the souls of everyone else on earth—whether they have been good to you or not. He wants you to be a constant giver of love, whether or not that love is deserved. When you were not deserving, I, the Son of God, sacrificed My life for you. Does it not make sense that God would want you to love others, regardless of whether it is deserved? Now that's crazy—but that's love!

" 'Love the Lord your God with all your passion and prayer and intelligence. . . . Love others as well as you love yourself.' These two commands are pegs; everything in God's Law and the Prophets hangs from them."
MATTHEW 22:37–40 MSG

Overflowing with Hope

Do you want the peace that surpasses all understanding? Then empty yourself of all worldly angst and worry. Put all your trust in Me. I am the One who can give you that amazing calmness, the One who can help you to sleep peacefully in the midst of a boat-rocking storm. This wonderful peace is a precursor to all-encompassing joy. And this joy and peace leads to an overabundance of hope!

It's available through the power of the Helper I sent to you thousands of years ago. That same power has not abated. That power was available to miracle workers of old—and is still available to you today. The same amount. The same strength. And you are the vessel for that power. All you need to do is trust your God, reach out, believe in Him, and He will fill you to overflowing with hope—all you need to lead a victorious life in Me. My greatest desire for you is that you live this blessed life to the fullest. Are you ready to have your cup runneth over?

May the God of hope fill you with all joy and peace as
you trust in him, so that you may overflow with
hope by the power of the Holy Spirit.
ROMANS 15:13 NIV

The Word

In the beginning was God. And He spoke things into being. His utterance, His Word, was Me. I have been around since the very beginning of time. Through Me, the world was made. For nothing was made until God spoke it (through Me, the Word) into existence. And with the help of the Holy Spirit, I continue to make God's thoughts clear to you through the written Word—that Bible you have before you. The precious book you hold in your hands.

As you read that Word, study it, and apply it to your life, you find yourself drawing closer and closer to God. The Word in action makes you more and more like Me. This Word is power. This Word is truth. This Word is the answer to every question you have in life. Take it to heart, for nothing is more precious, more powerful, and more perfect.

In the beginning [before all time] was the Word (Christ),
and the Word was with God, and the Word was God Himself.
He was [continually existing] in the beginning [co-eternally]
with God. All things were made and came into existence
through Him; and without Him not even one thing
was made that has come into being.

JOHN 1:1–3 AMP

Purpose-Filled Promises

The Bible is not full of empty promises. No! It is full of powerful words—words that have been sent to accomplish God's purpose on heaven and on earth. Everything that He has said, all that He and I have promised, has an effect on the spiritual and the physical world. Scripture is alive, able to do everything from defeating evil, spreading peace, melting hearts, dividing and uniting kingdoms, subduing enemies, and toppling terrorists to changing lives, making dreams a reality, producing prosperity, strengthening marriages, raising children, abating sorrow, and more. From things mighty to things small, God's Word, His promises, are packed with power. There is no detail too small but God's promises have it covered. From the slightest worry to the most life-altering challenge, God's promises apply. And there is nothing so great that the Word cannot conquer. So search the Word. Find a promise to apply to your life. And witness the power and purpose of the words that have come forth from His mouth to man's ear to your heart.

"So will My word be which goes out of My mouth;
it will not return to Me void (useless, without result),
without accomplishing what I desire, and without
succeeding in the matter for which I sent it."
Isaiah 55:11 amp

Ready Help

I know all that is going on in your life. So please, do not try to hide yourself away. Instead, bring all your shame and troubles to Me. I am so ready to lift you above all your sorrows. I too have lived in your world. I have felt the pain and affliction it can bring. But I have also experienced the world's joys and triumphs.

So let go of all the chains that keep you from coming to Me. Break through all the self-made barriers that would have you cower in the dark. Step out of that dungeon and into the light of My presence. Walk right up and take what I am ready to give you. I have more mercy, love, kindness, and strength than you could ever imagine. And there is no one I would rather help than you, no one I would rather lift up than you, and no one I would rather love than you, for I see who you really are and who you are about to be.

Now that we know what we have—Jesus, this great High Priest with ready access to God—let's not let it slip through our fingers. We don't have a priest who is out of touch with our reality. He's been through weakness and testing, experienced it all—all but the sin. So let's walk right up to him and get what he is so ready to give. Take the mercy, accept the help.
Hebrews 4:14–16 msg

Certain as the Dawn

Each and every day, return to Me. Read My Word to understand Me. Recognize when My hand is shaping and molding your life. Look for Me in unexpected places—in the flowers that bloom, the snow that falls, the river that winds, and the breeze that caresses your cheek. See Me in the eyes of a child, the kiss of a loved one, the scent on the air, the sun on your face, the flight of a bird, the joy in your heart.

I am in and all around you, keeping you safe, whispering in your ear, shielding you from danger, leading you through the labyrinth of life. You will find no better guide or teacher than Me and My Word. Learn us. Know us. Appreciate and cherish us. For we are one and the same. We are unstoppable. Like the streams that change the face of the earth over time, I am the Living Water that is helping you to carve out a godly life—for you and the children after you. As One who never changes, I will always come to you, certain as the dawn.

"Come and let us return [in repentance] to the LORD. . . .
Let us know and become personally acquainted with Him;
let us press on to know and understand fully the [greatness of the]
LORD [to honor, heed, and deeply cherish Him]. His appearing is
prepared and is as certain as the dawn, and He will come
to us [in salvation] like the [heavy] rain, like the
spring rain watering the earth."

HOSEA 6:1, 3 AMP

To Serve with Love

Dear sister, I ask you to follow My example. Serve others with love—whether they have asked you to or not. Will you do so? Do you do so? When I was with My disciples, I got down on My knees to wash their feet. In so doing, I hoped they would see how they were to serve each other—no questions asked. And to allow others to serve them—no questions asked.

So do not protest when those you feel are "above" you seek to serve you. Allow them to experience the joy of a servant's heart. Do not try to pay them back, but allow them to feel the selfless love they have given you. Then go and do the same for some other soul. Without being asked, serve with love, compassion, desire, humility, and grace. Such an act on your knees will raise your spirit high—in this world and the next.

"Now that I, your Lord and Teacher, have washed your feet, you also should wash one another's feet. I have set you an example that you should do as I have done for you. Very truly I tell you, no servant is greater than his master, nor is a messenger greater than the one who sent him. Now that you know these things, you will be blessed if you do them."
JOHN 13:14–17 NIV

Rise Up!

Just when things look like they won't get any better, just when the cold and darkness seem to be swallowing you whole, remember Me. Come away with Me. Rise above the sorrows of this world. Like spring, I have come to warm your heart and lighten your load. In My presence, the winters of life hold no power—and the certainty of spring is on the rise. With Me, you can bloom where you are planted, no matter what the earthly season. You will hear the voice of the birds who live to sing praises in My name.

This is your season. This is your spring. This is your period of renewal, joy, warmth, and light. Let Me see your face, hear your voice. Know that when you are with Me, winter becomes a vague memory. So raise your arms and lift them up to the Son.

My beloved spoke, and said to me: "Rise up, my love, my fair one, and come away. For lo, the winter is past, the rain is over and gone. The flowers appear on the earth; the time of singing has come, and the voice of the turtledove is heard in our land."
SONG OF SOLOMON 2:10–12 NKJV

Live, Laugh, Love

Yes, there is trouble in your world—on the spiritual and material planes. But as I have told you before, "I have overcome the world!" So don't allow the doom and gloom to settle on your heart. Don't let each and every piece of bad news destroy your triumphant outlook. You are My followers—so rejoice! Even if you don't feel like smiling, smile anyway. And before you know it, it will be a continual habit.

Take some time out of each and every day to play, to lose yourself in the simple, easy things. In the privacy of your home, spin, twirl, skip. Before you know it, you will be laughing like a child. Such a lift will be a gift to your heart. Earthly life is too short to be weighed down by wars, murders, terrorists, fires, and all other calamities. You were never meant to hear and bear the news of an entire world—or even your own little piece of it. So stop the madness. Live, laugh, love. It does a body—and soul—good.

A cheerful disposition is good for your health;
gloom and doom leave you bone-tired.
PROVERBS 17:22 MSG

On the Other Side

I know the pain you are feeling. I too shed tears for those who passed on from one world to the next. But trust Me. You will see them again one day. After all, I have promised this to you. There is a place that I have set aside for each and every believer. So do not worry about them leaving you behind. They will be waiting for you on the other side. And when your time comes, you will be reunited with them—forever.

In the meantime, know that this hurt shall eventually fade away. Nothing can really ever separate you from the love you had for that person and the love he or she had for you. Hold the richness of that thought in your heart. And remember the mansion that awaits in the sky for the followers of God's light and Word.

"Don't let this throw you. You trust God, don't you? Trust me. There is plenty of room for you in my Father's home. If that weren't so, would I have told you that I'm on my way to get a room ready for you? And if I'm on my way to get your room ready, I'll come back and get you so you can live where I live."
JOHN 14:1–3 MSG

Precious Lamb

You are My precious lamb. There are so many things you have yet to discover, so many lessons you have yet to learn, so many paths you have yet to travel with Me. So follow closely. Spend time in My presence. Then you will learn to know and recognize My voice when I speak. You will be familiar with My promptings, those sparks of divine intuition, inspiration, and ideas. There will be a wonderful connection between My Spirit and yours. You will more easily be led to where I am guiding you.

Yes, learn My voice—every word, inflection, tone, and correction. Do not lose the import of what I say to you. Become so familiar with My way, My light, and My spark that you will be able to know Me, your Shepherd, in the flash of an eye and obey Me just as quickly, even when amid a crowded flock.

"My sheep hear My voice, and I know them, and they follow Me. And I give them eternal life, and they shall never perish; neither shall anyone snatch them out of My hand. My Father, who has given them to Me, is greater than all; and no one is able to snatch them out of My Father's hand. I and My Father are one."
JOHN 10:27–30 NKJV

God's Eyes

Are you doing whatever you think is right in your own eyes? If so, what weights are you using on your scale of rightness and wrongness? What is your litmus test?

In the days of the judges, there were no kings in Israel. So everyone did what *he* thought was right—and chaos ensued. But you, dear sister, have a King in your life—He is God the Father. He is looking at what you are doing, discerning your true motive, and testing your heart. Is it in line with His will for your life? Have you determined if it meets the parameters of the great commandment—to love God, yourself, and others? If you are ever in doubt, stop. Come to Me. Ask Me to reveal your true intents, your heart, the purpose behind your actions. Ask Me to allow you to take a step back, to see things with God's perspective, to remove the scales from your eyes. Come outside of yourself to see within yourself and the truth that lies there. Then, once you are certain that your will is in line with God's, continue on with Our blessings.

We justify our actions by appearances;
GOD examines our motives.
PROVERBS 21:2 MSG

Magic Elixir

In your world, your time in My presence is a magic elixir for the soul. That calmness and contentment you gain is what keeps the spirit and the bones healthy. Stop trying to get everything under your control. Those efforts are futile—and lead only to an early demise. Instead, acknowledge that you are grateful just going where I lead, knowing that I will equip you for every task for which I have given you an urging.

Quiet your soul as you come into My presence. Like a baby who no longer needs milk from her mother's breast, be happy where you are. Allow your heart to be at peace. Let the pressures and conflicts of this particular time in your life fade away into nothing. Rest in My arms where there is nothing but light and a gentleness beyond compare. Let Me hold you, stroke your hair, whisper a lullaby. Rest, secure in Me. Then wait and hope, today and all the days to come.

GOD, I'm not trying to rule the roost, I don't want to be king of the mountain. . . . I've kept my feet on the ground, I've cultivated a quiet heart. Like a baby content in its mother's arms, my soul is a baby content. Wait, Israel, for GOD. Wait with hope. Hope now; hope always!
PSALM 131:1–3 MSG

Perseverance

You have come up against many obstacles in your efforts to complete an endeavor. You have suffered many trials. Come to Me for whatever extra energy and courage you need to finish the task at hand. Know that with My help, you can do anything. Know that I am working within you to help you bring things to completion. Never doubt for a second that this thing will be done.

You have the talent. You have the drive. You have the vision. You have the determination. You have the will. And I have given you the way. So do not despair but keep on keeping on. Persevere against all odds and you will be rewarded, for you have put feet to your faith. And that always makes Me smile, for it tends to make unbelievers gasp.

This is to your advantage, who were the first to begin a year ago not only to take action. . .but also [the first] to desire to do it. So now finish this, so that your eagerness in desiring it may be equaled by your completion of it, according to your ability.
2 Corinthians 8:10–11 amp

Heart's Desires

What are the desires of your heart? To find your true love? Have children? Have a successful career? Serve others? Become a surgeon? Graduate from law school? Or are you uncertain as to which road to take in any of those life directions?

If you are not sure what your true desire is, come to Me as a young girl to her big brother. Sit next to Me and ask whatever questions you will. I will answer. Together we will discover your true desire. Perhaps it was a dream you gave up long ago. Perhaps it was a childhood wish that you never thought possible. Whatever it is, you will discover and obtain that which you were designed to be when you seek out and enjoy the presence of My Father and Me. All secrets will be revealed. All desires will be met. All dreams will become reality. That is the work and will of My Father and Me. Come. Discover a new place, a new life, a new dream, a new way, a new joy with Us.

Delight yourself in the LORD, and He will give you the desires and petitions of your heart.
PSALM 37:4 AMP

Let Peace Reign

Your heart is thumping. Tears begin to well up in your eyes. To hide the fact that your fists are clenching and unclenching, you fold your arms in front of your chest. When your teeth begin to clamp together, you realize that this is not the time to make a decision. That's the light from Me. That's My prompt, telling you to get out while the getting is good. To extract yourself from the current situation. To come and seek My face.

If you allow Me, I will give you the peace you need before you speak. I will give you the wisdom you need to make the right decision, to help your heart and your mind come to the right conclusion. So, when your emotions threaten to take control, run—into My arms! Give Me your anger, your tears, your stress, your troubles. And I will help you give My peace the reins.

Let the peace of Christ [the inner calm of one who walks daily with Him] be the controlling factor in your hearts [deciding and settling questions that arise]. To this peace indeed you were called as members in one body [of believers].
COLOSSIANS 3:15 AMP

Resurrection Power

Do not worry about the power of temptation. Do not see the things that plague you as forces that cannot be overcome. Do not be concerned about the limited vision you have in certain areas of your life. Forget about all the issues, problems, and, sometimes, people that seem to weigh you down. God sent Me to help you. He has given Me all the power I need to break you out of any spiritual, emotional, financial, physical, and mental prison you are in. He has given Me the healing power to restore your sight. He has given Me the strength to carry whatever burdens you are bearing. He has given Me the keenness of mind to deliver you from unhealthy relationships.

Simply come to Me, knowing that I, whom God raised from the trappings of death, am going to change your life. I am going to raise you from whatever binds you. Trust in that resurrection power. . . . I am your example that anything is possible. Trust in Me.

God's Spirit is on me; he's chosen me to preach the Message of good news to the poor, sent me to announce pardon to prisoners and recovery of sight to the blind, to set the burdened and battered free, to announce, "This is God's year to act!"
Luke 4:18–19 msg

Uplifting Praise

Lift your arms in praise, like a tree stretching to meet Me in the sky. Open your arms wide to capture the blessings of sunshine, rain, and snow. Raise your face, basking in the glow of My light, the power of My words, the cleansing of My touch. Open your heart to the love I am ready to lavish upon you. Allow it to fill your entire being, leaving no corner untouched. Allow it to heal every disappointment, hurt, sorrow, and pain you have endured. Open up your soul to the truth I am waiting to set upon you. Allow it to expand your vision, until you see Me in every part of your life. Open up your spirit to hear My voice loud and clear. Allow it to change you from the inside out, making you more and more like Me. Lift your entire being up to our Father. Be glad in all you are, in all that He has made you to be. Share the joy We bring to you, today and every day. Let not your heart ever be troubled. Let the sweetness of His name, His works, and His blessings overflow from His arms into yours.

May the glory of the LORD endure forever; may the LORD rejoice in His works. . . . I will sing to the LORD as long as I live; I will sing praise to my God while I have my being. May my meditation be sweet to Him; I will be glad in the LORD.
PSALM 104:31, 33–34 NKJV

The Ultimate Weapon

Thoughts are flitting through your mind all the time. They ricochet from one corner of your brain to another. Fortunately, you were not designed to follow every idea that comes into your head. If you did, you'd be going in a thousand different directions at once. That's because it's only the thoughts you claim that have the real power. And the more you own them—the longer you let them linger—the more powerful they get. Over time, these claimed thoughts grow feet, arms, and legs and take on a life of their own.

That is why you need to take all thoughts captive and bring them into My light. Test them against My Word. Realize that they are only thoughts, after all. Using My strength, My Word, you can regain control. The power you have in Me—that is your ultimate weapon. That is how you can change your thoughts, which will in turn change your mind, your life, and the world.

The weapons we fight with are not the weapons of the world.
On the contrary, they have divine power to demolish strongholds.
We demolish arguments and every pretension that sets itself
up against the knowledge of God, and we take captive
every thought to make it obedient to Christ.

2 CORINTHIANS 10:4–5 NIV

A Door Wide Open

I am calling you to a new space, a new area, a new opportunity, a new endeavor where you will do mighty things. Are your ears open? Do you hear My voice? Are you ready to glorify God—or is something holding you back? Others initially refused their call. Moses didn't think he was a good enough speaker to talk for God. Jonah initially refused to tackle the mission Father God had for him—so he became bait and was swallowed by a large fish. Then there was Gideon, whom the angel of God addressed as a mighty warrior while he was still a farmer threshing grain.

Dare to believe that I am calling you. That although a new path may seem scary, it is the right path. That I will not send you out ill-equipped. Break free from the fetters of your comfortable world. Stop listening to the lies that you aren't good enough, smart enough, strong enough. You are a woman who, when she makes up her mind to, can accomplish anything with Me. I am holding the door wide open. Walk through to a new life.

Because a wide door for effective service has opened
to me [in Ephesus, a very promising opportunity],
and there are many adversaries.
1 CORINTHIANS 16:9 AMP

Loved Ones

I am here, ready and waiting. Bring your loved ones before Me. No words need to be said. I can read your mind's desire for each one. I can discern your heart's concerns, pick up on your hopes, see your dreams, and feel your love for each one of them. They are precious in your sight—and Mine. Bring them before Me, and then let them go, one by one. Put them into My care and leave them here. Know that I will do what's best for them.

The love you show as a mother, wife, sister, aunt, grandmother, friend, and fellow believer warms My heart. And the faith that you have in Me, to leave all your worries and what-ifs in My capable hands, puts a smile on My face. Allow Me to hold this burden for you. You have done what you could. You have revealed the wonder and truth of your faith. You are demonstrating both to those you love, and they will be the richer for it. May your faith continue to umpteen generations.

That precious memory triggers another: your honest faith—and what a rich faith it is, handed down from your grandmother Lois to your mother Eunice, and now to you!
2 TIMOTHY 1:5 MSG

Heart Dreams

What are the dreams you hold in your heart, in that secret place deep, deep down where you commit your most precious thoughts? Tell Me, tell Me all. I want to know what you yearn for. I want to hear what path you would like to take in My name. I want to understand what you are thinking, how much you trust Me, how willing you are to just take things day by day.

I am here to remind you to honor your dreams that I have planted in your heart. They are there for a reason—because you are the only one who can live that dream. A space in time has been carved out for you. Are you willing to seek it, to fill the void no one else can? Honor your dreams. Make a space for them in your life. And then, when you find your path, when you are completely satisfied to take what I give you day to day and then trust Me—and only Me—for the rest, amazing things will begin to happen. Follow your dreams. Then once you are on your road, help to honor the dreams of others. Help them realize their goals—and glorify Me!

May He grant you your heart's desire and fulfill all your plans. . . . Some trust in chariots and some in horses, but we will remember and trust in the name of the LORD our God.
PSALM 20:4, 7 AMP

Time of Testing

As I was tested in the Garden of Gethsemane, so you will have times of testing in your own life. Do not worry about these seasons, for I will always be there to help you bear up under them, as Father God helped Me. I even asked Him if He would take the cup from Me. But He did not. And after the pain and torture, I ended up saving the world, rising again in God's amazing power.

You too can request help and clarity from God—but know that if a time of trial is God's will and way, He will give you the help to bear up under it. He will give you the strength to do what He has given you to do. And you too will see the amazing joy and victory when your testing is over. For you will have learned how to endure, how to ride the wave with God through every tempest and storm.

Dear. . .sisters, when troubles of any kind come your way, consider it an opportunity for great joy. For you know that when your faith is tested, your endurance has a chance to grow. So let it grow, for when your endurance is fully developed, you will be perfect and complete, needing nothing.
JAMES 1:2–4 NLT

Shallow-End Advice

Time and time again, Father God and I have saved you from your enemies—seen and unseen. We have kept you from being snared by the evil one. We have given you a way out when you were faced by temptation. We put a hedge of protection around you when you begged for Us to shield you from harm. In these times of danger, you breathed the words, "Jesus, help me!" and I immediately responded. Afterward, your heart still pounding, you were praising Us over and over again. Yet the next day you'd forgotten all about what We had done for you! Sister, may this not be so!

Remember Our promises! Remember how often We have saved you from yourself and others. Keep all these rescues in mind once you are safe. But do not become complacent. And above all, don't run headlong into another sticky situation. Stop! Wait! Ask for My help before your next move. Call on Me while you're still in the shallow end—not ready to jump off the high dive. Stop. Wait. Ask. Then follow Our advice. Remember Our promises. Then you will praise Our name!

[The Lord] rescued them from their enemies. . . . Then his people believed his promises. Then they sang his praise. Yet how quickly they forgot what he had done! They wouldn't wait for his counsel! In the wilderness their desires ran wild, testing God's patience in that dry wasteland.
PSALM 106:10, 12–14 NLT

Pouring Out

Tell Me all that is on your mind. Hold nothing back! Pour your heart and soul out to Me. Let your armor drop. Let your guard down. Allow nothing to stand between us—no weapon, no shield, no shame. Enough of the brave front, the facade, the mask that you wear in front of so many others. Show Me the true you. I will not turn you away. I will not mock you. Instead, I want to know you. I crave to know exactly what is going on in your life.

There is no need for you to sugarcoat anything. Believe Me—I have heard it all, so nothing you say is going to shock Me. Let's talk together. Let's get it all down to the bare bones so we can build your life up again. There is no need to fear Me. Simply come. Talk. And pour out your soul. I am here to receive all that you say, all that you are, all that you have been—and help fill you up again.

But Hannah answered and said, "No, my lord, I am a woman of sorrowful spirit. I have drunk neither wine nor intoxicating drink, but have poured out my soul before the LORD. Do not consider your maidservant a wicked woman, for out of the abundance of my complaint and grief I have spoken until now."
1 SAMUEL 1:15–16 NKJV

Remember Lot's Wife

How willing are you to follow Me? What are you willing to leave behind on the material plane to become closer to Me on the spiritual plane? How much are you willing to sacrifice so you can truly move forward?

Each and every day you have a choice to make—to come with Me down the path I have laid out for you or to stay where you are, no matter what the consequences. It's all up to you. If you disregard My pleas and stay on the plane of your current existence, you may just end up stuck there, wondering where your opportunity went. But if you decide to listen to Me, to follow My lead, you will find yourself going forward to the mountain, continually rising up higher and higher, closer and closer to God and the kingdom of heaven.

Perhaps you may start out with Me but then, longing for what had been, look back at what you've left behind. Chances are, that constant looking back will bring not only discontentment but more trouble in the long run. So decide. What are you going to do—walk with Me, eyes looking forward, or look back at your own peril?

When they had brought them outside, one [of the angels] said, "Escape for your life! Do not look behind you, or stop anywhere in the entire valley; escape to the mountains [of Moab], or you will be consumed and swept away". . . . But Lot's wife, from behind him, [foolishly, longingly] looked [back toward Sodom in an act of disobedience], and she became a pillar of salt.

GENESIS 19:17, 26 AMP

God Space

The diaper pile seems to be growing by the moment. Your new job is asking for more responsibility—but offering less pay. You're not sure you've got anything to cook for dinner tonight, but you're too tired to stop at the store. The weekend you had planned to get away has been canceled—due to your having to nurse a sick husband. There seems to be no time, no energy, no you left.

I too had My fill of work thousands of years ago. My days were spent preaching, teaching, healing, and blessing one person after another. But I knew how to recharge. I would walk away from the crowds and find My own space to be alone with God our Father—many more times than the Bible notes. Where do you go to get refueled by God? Where do you go to regain your strength, compassion, energy, and love? Carve out your own wilderness in life. Make a space that will be occupied by you and God—alone. Then take off your mask. Come face-to-face with your Maker. Pray for His touch of healing, love, and guidance. Rest as long as need be. But come. Don't delay.

But despite Jesus' instructions, the report of his power spread even faster, and vast crowds came to hear him preach and to be healed of their diseases. But Jesus often withdrew to the wilderness for prayer.
Luke 5:15–16 nlt